THEN & NOW

VENTURA

OPPOSITE: A pastoral view taken from above Poli Street shows a very rural Ventura in the 1890s. Plaza School dominates the corner of Santa Clara and Fir Streets across from Plaza Park, and ships are next to the Ventura Wharf. Off to the right is the massive Rose Hotel, which was located at the corner of Main and Chestnut Streets. (Bill Appleton.)

THEN & NOW

VENTURA

Glenda J. Jackson

This book is dedicated to my family.

Library of Congress Control Number: 2009928055

Published by Arcadia Publishing
Charleston SC, Chicago IL, Portsmouth NH, San Francisco CA

Printed in the United States of America

For all general information contact Arcadia Publishing at:
Telephone 843-853-2070
Fax 843-853-0044
E-mail sales@arcadiapublishing.com
For customer service and orders:
Toll-Free 1-888-313-2665

Visit us on the Internet at www.arcadiapublishing.com

ON THE FRONT COVER: Main Street, looking east in the 1890s, is filled with the hustle and bustle of people, horses, buggies, and a family posing for an unidentified photographer. Note the Livestock Slaughtering Company sign on a storefront building. An early city ordinance required the slaughterhouses to dispose of carcasses in the ocean near the mouth of the Ventura River. The large building beyond the mission is the Anacapa Hotel, and in the distance, the spire of its competitor, the Rose Hotel, is plainly seen. (Author.)

ON THE BACK COVER: The Rose Hotel, built during the 1880s railroad boom, looms at the corner of Chestnut and Main Streets. This 1895 photograph of Main Street looking west shows the top of the Anacapa Hotel and the mission bell tower visible in the distance. East Main Street would have been out in the boonies, since Ventura was predominantly farmland beyond this point. Both the Anacapa and Rose Hotels were built to cater to the tourist trade. (Bill Appleton.)

CONTENTS

ACKNOWLEDGMENTS

I have many people to thank for making my third book a reality. A huge thank you to all the past historians who documented Ventura's stories so well! I would also like to thank the E. P. Foster Library for allowing me access to the old editions of the local newspapers. I am forever indebted to everyone who allowed me access to their private collections of photographs. I would like to especially thank Don Taylor, who volunteered to run around town with me and take the "now" photographs.

PHOTO CREDITS
THEN IMAGE SOURCES:
Bill Appleton, 28, 31, 36
Eric Daily, 12, 23, 24, 43, 53, 69, 77
Don Mills, 18
Robin Blanchard, 19, 40, 56
Dena Mercer, 20, 84
Craig Held, 26, 45, 47, 49, 52, 63, 64, 67, 70, 75, 79
Terry Chaffee, 27, 42, 44, 72
Collection of Merrill Allyn, 32, 34, 35
Shirley Weeks, 39
Linda Stallard, 41
Richard W. Mills, 50
Shawna Atchison, 51
Olivas Adobe Historical Interpreters, 62, 93–95
Marcie Maloney, 71, 83
Jerry D. Hamilton, 76, 78
San Buenaventura Heritage Association, 85, 87–92
Charles Cole Jr., 86
The author provided all other then images.

NOW IMAGE SOURCES:
Don Taylor, 12–14, 17–19, 21, 23, 24, 27, 28, 32, 35, 38–48, 50, 51, 53–63, 66–69, 71, 72
The author provided all other now images.

INTRODUCTION

"Ventura has many charms that attract the stranger. Your city impresses me as being alive; its people proud of its cleanliness and order. I am delighted with the place." Thus speaks George W. Andrus, a retired attorney of Oak Park, Illinois, who has come here to reside. He has taken the Vandever cottage and will probably remain here indefinitely. Andrus visited the coast last year and, passing through Ventura, stopped here for a day. He was so pleased with our city that upon reaching his home he ordered the Free Press to be sent to him and has kept in touch with it ever since. Returning to California, he came directly to our city by the sea. He finds many things to please and delight him here. The balmy climate, the soft cool air from the sea, the wealth of flowers, the quiet, restful surroundings, and the beautiful location of Ventura all charm him. He compliments Ventura on the progressive spirit so noticeable to the newcomer and thinks the town has a great future.

—*Ventura Free Press*, April 21, 1909

So it was 100 years ago, and so it is now. People have made observations about Ventura as far back as 1602, such as Spanish navigator Sebastian Vizcaino, who named the Santa Barbara Channel. And we continue to make observations and unearth Ventura's historical treasures—whether it is the tiniest photograph of Chinatown or perhaps sitting down and reminiscing with a Venturan who has lived here for 80 years. What I personally enjoy is the minute detail: the background scenery in a photograph (the buildings and street signs); the person sitting in a buggy; the roofline of a house or the ridgelines of our mountains. The quest for history continues. That is what is so unique about Ventura—when you peel back one layer, it reveals another.

Putting together this book has been an interesting project. Sometimes getting the same angle for a photograph was impossible due to the development that has taken place, with large housing tracts obscuring what was a bird's-eye view in the 1880s. Sometimes it was a stand of trees that grew over the course of 80 years. But sometimes luck prevailed, such as on the way down Brakey Road from Grant Park (grumbling about those trees), when an "open house" presented the perfect opportunity. Camera in hand, we looked at the condo and stepped out on the balcony to grab the shot. I was also proud of myself for not falling down the hill behind the mission to capture the now image of the quadrangle. I did, however, decide against traipsing through tall scrub brush for fear of snakes. For some photographs, the only way to identify a then image was the ridgeline of the mountains in the background. I have gotten quite good at this little detail. But before I digress any further, I would like to provide a little background on Ventura.

It is hard to imagine that from a small cluster of old adobe houses around Mission San Buenaventura, Ventura has grown into a large metropolitan city of over 115,000 residents. Situated on the Central Coast, our Mediterranean climate and wide-open space lured settlers here and proved to be fertile ground both for cultivation of flowers and crops and for oil production. The adobes have crumbled away, replaced by business districts and houses. The farmland, once covering the majority of the town, has been replaced with housing developments. Fortunately, not all the farmland has been lost. Traveling through East Ventura along Telegraph Road, it is refreshing to pass orchards planted in citrus and avocado. Local farmers' markets are crowded with weekend shoppers enjoying the bounty offered in Ventura County. On any given weekend, our local beaches are crowded, even in stormy weather, with visitors and residents alike.

Having lived in Ventura for over 30 years, I have come to enjoy the "June Gloom," what I consider traffic (although honestly it is nothing compared to Los Angeles), and the fact that in this metropolitan city we have red-tailed hawks, egrets, raccoons, possums, and ground squirrels in the oddest of places. I hope people will take this book and visit the various locations to learn a little bit more about Ventura—then and now.

THE MISSION AND OLD TOWN

Ventura, Cal., in 1875.

The wagon and buggy are traveling west on Main Street toward Chestnut Street in this scene from 1875. Cattle drives were common through town, along with the occasional runaway buggy.

The wooden cages protected tree saplings from wandering livestock. Always visible in the distance for miles around is the bell tower of the Mission San Bonaventura.

Mission San Buenaventura draws thousands of visitors annually. Named after Saint Bonaventure, this mission was an extremely successful and prosperous mission. Boasting elaborate gardens and extensive orchards with many types of exotic fruits grown on the grounds, the mission was actually the first to grow oranges on the West Coast. The vintage photograph dates to approximately the 1870s and is one of the earliest images of the mission known to exist. Today the mission operates as a parish church with a very large congregation.

THE MISSION AND THE OLD TOWN

San Buenaventura Mission.　　Ventura, Cal.

PUBL. BY
MACGREGOR BROS

This vintage image shows the location of the old cemetery west of the mission. Today Holy Cross School sits on the site. The construction of this church was started around 1792 and was completed in 1809. An earthquake in 1812 severely damaged the building, and it reopened in 1815.

Today's view of the mission is obscured by the towering Norfolk pines that were planted in the 1870s. The vintage image shows very young trees, the parish house, and a small museum building adjacent to the church. The parish house is long gone, and the museum has moved to the right of the courtyard, housing many mission artifacts, including the pulpit, old doors, and remnants of two of the wooden bells that hung in the bell tower.

THE MISSION AND THE OLD TOWN

The mission quadrangle provided protection and housed workshops for the Chumash Indians to learn trades such as leather tanning and weaving.

In order to get the same angle, a little derring-do was required by going in and around a fence and not falling down the hill.

OLD SAN BUENAVENTURA MISSION, FOUNDED 1782. VENTURA, CAL.

In order to survive, the mission needed large quantities of water for its lush gardens and orchards as well as for drinking and washing clothes. A 7-mile-long aqueduct was constructed beginning near present-day Oakview. The vintage postcard image shows the aqueduct remnant off Highway 33 and Canada Larga Road. The now image was taken from the opposite side and shows the damage that occurred in a severe flooding incident in 2005.

Stone Ditch, Built by the Indians over 130 Years Ago, Ventura, Cal.

THE MISSION AND THE OLD TOWN

Few people know that this settling tank, El Caballo, exists in Eastwood Park below Poli Street. The water spout resembled a horse's head, hence its name. The tank filtered water that traveled miles down the aqueduct. A Chumash Indian would operate levers to divert the water to the mission below or to the gardens. The tank was also Ventura's first jail. One story has it that a drunk was tossed in with a black bear. The bear won.

THE MISSION AND THE OLD TOWN

The vintage image of the Tico Adobe dates to the late 1890s. Many adobes such as this one once lined Main Street. Adobe bricks were formed from mud mixed with straw and horse manure then left to dry and harden over the course of several months. To protect the adobes from water, they would be whitewashed with a mixture that included ground seashells. Today Burger King is at that location, Main Street and Ventura Avenue.

The Ortega Adobe is located on West Main Street not far from the Tico Adobe location. Constructed in 1859, it was home to the Ortegas, a family of 13, and was saved from destruction by a local women's league in 1911. The City of Ventura owns the Ortega, and it is open to the public for self-guided tours. It is the birthplace of the Ortega Chili Packing Company, and today people still purchase Ortega green chiles in the supermarket.

Ventura's Chinatown was a cluster of wooden shanty buildings on Figueroa Street between Main and Santa Clara Streets, directly below the mission. The earliest known arrival in Ventura is approximately 1865. The Chinese suffered greatly from discrimination, although their fire company was highly regarded and often on the scene before the local fire brigade. In 2004, highly respected Chinese artists Qi Pang and Guo SongYun painted a mural in China Alley honoring Ventura's Chinese.

The vintage image dates to the mid-1890s and shows the shanties that the Chinese lived in. The poor little children are scared witless by the lady with the box camera. Approximately 200 Chinese lived in the cluster of wooden buildings on Figueroa Street.

This is Colombo Street, a very short and short-lived street between Main and Santa Clara Streets. The buildings in the distance are the Ventura County Courthouse (brick) and Ventura County Hospital (white clapboard). These buildings sat on mission orchard land donated by the Catholic Church to the newly formed County of Ventura. The courthouse was built in 1875 and torn down around 1910. The two palms were the last vestiges of the mission gardens. The now image was taken looking across Mission Park.

THE MISSION AND THE OLD TOWN

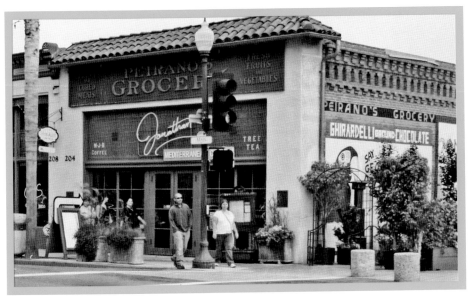

As more people arrived to town, the old adobes gave way to commercial buildings, such as Gandolfo's Market, built in the 1870s. In 1890, it became Peirano's, a mainstay in downtown Ventura for over 100 years. The store has been renovated and now operates as an upscale restaurant—Jonathan's at Peirano's.

The vintage photograph shows stores east of Gandolfo's. It is believed that this building is the first commercial brick building constructed in Ventura. Today a variety of retail shops, including boutiques, thrift stores, and eateries, occupy this block. It is hard to imagine that in the 1870s, residents would have enjoyed bullfights a mere two blocks away.

THE MISSION AND THE OLD TOWN

Anacapa Hotel.   VENTURA, Cal.

The Anacapa Hotel, on the corner of Main and Palm Streets, was built in 1888 by Fridolin Hartman. Boasting electric lights and over 120 rooms, it was a major competitor of the Rose Hotel and was torn down in the 1920s. The Top Hat burger stand was built sometime in the 1940s or 1950s. Ventura will once again lose an eclectic landmark when this entire parcel is redeveloped.

An 1880s marching band, forever frozen in place, heads south on Palm Street toward Santa Clara Street; the reason for the celebration is lost in history. The first Fourth of July celebration was in 1860. Today an antique mall operates out of the old Woolworth's Store on the corner of Main and Palm Streets.

THE MISSION AND THE OLD TOWN

Chaffee Dry Goods Store, established in 1863, stood on the corner of Palm and Main Streets. Walter Chaffee was the first mayor of the city of San Buenaventura and a local merchant. Chaffee Dry Goods was the largest mercantile in town and remained in the family until 1929, when it became the Ventura Department Store. An advertisement from 1895 advertises dry goods, clothing, furnishings, shoes, groceries, and hardware. The site today houses a bank.

The vintage bird's-eye view of Ventura shows Palm Street heading south to the ocean. The large building to the right is the back of the Anacapa Hotel. Bird's-eye view photographs are invaluable to local historians and show the change that has taken place.

THE MISSION AND THE OLD TOWN

CHAPTER 2

DOWN BY THE SEASHORE

Beach Scene, Ventura, Cal.

This vintage postcard shows a typical day at the beach not unlike today. Thousands of people flock each year to Ventura's sandy shores, even braving June Gloom. People and families head to the beach to sunbathe, surf, fish, wade in the surf, or to just enjoy a leisurely walk on the old pier.

VENTURA BATH HOUSE, VENTURA, CALIFORNIA.

The old Ventura Bath House was opened in 1918 and featured an indoor pool filled with seawater on the main floor and a dance floor on the second floor. After several years, the pool was covered over and turned into a skate rink. The Ventura Bath House was torn down around 1957. Today the site contains this large parking structure.

The Ventura Wharf was built in 1872 and has been an iconic attraction ever since. Originally designed for commercial trade, ships mooring alongside the wharf were a common sight. Turning more into a recreational pier in the 1930s, residents and tourists still stroll along the wooden deck to enjoy the sea air or a day of fishing. The author's grandson, Julian Ponce, enjoys getting his feet wet in the now image.

The 1950s image shows Shore Drive, which used to run along the beach. The bathhouse is visible in the background, and the Chaffee House is on the corner. California Street ended at Shore Drive, and before the freeway came through, it was an easy walk down to the beach. Shore Drive no longer exists, and Crowne Plaza Hotel stands where the Chaffee House once stood.

Due to Ventura's geographical makeup, thick marine layers and fog banks are common. This unusual *c.* 1950 image shows a fog bank so thick it looks like smoke from a fire. The now image was taken on a clear day, and Anacapa Island, the nearest of the Channel Islands, is easily seen.

This early 1950s view from the Ventura Pier shows the bluffs that once were so prominent. Shore Drive (now Harbor Boulevard) runs along the beach and hidden behind the thick landscaping is the Pierpont Inn.

At one time, large petroleum tanks dotted the bluffs above the beach in Ventura, and oil lines snaked down the shore to the wharf and some ran beneath the water. Oil tankers anchored off the coast and filled their holds with rich crude oil from the underwater oil lines. A more common sight today is recreational boats or the jet skiers, as seen in the now photograph.

Ventura welcomed the iron horse in 1887. According to the caption on the photograph, this 1891 photograph shows crowds of people awaiting the arrival of Pres. Benjamin Harrison. Sitting below Front Street at the end of Kalorama Street, the train depot was a mainstay until it was unceremoniously torn down in the 1970s. The city had an opportunity to purchase it from Southern Pacific Railroad for $1 but declined.

CHAPTER 3

IN AND AROUND DOWNTOWN

Court House Ventura Calif.

When the 1875 county courthouse was condemned around 1909, seven sites were considered for a new courthouse. The *Ventura Free Press* reported, "There is an elegant hill site which is finding favor right at the head of California Street. It would head the most beautiful of our cross streets." In 1913, the Beaux-Arts–style courthouse opened with grand celebrations during a Fourth of July triple dedication that included the Ventura River Bridge and the opening of the causeway.

The Ventura County Courthouse became Ventura City Hall in 1974. This 1930s image shows the venerable Union National Bank on the right and the Ventura Hotel on the left. The structure just beyond the bank is the remodeled 1910 Athene Clubhouse. The bank still remains on the corner, albeit greatly modified, and a parking lot replaced the clubhouse.

IN AND AROUND DOWNTOWN

Finnish-born sculptor John Palo Kangas (on the scaffold) was commissioned to sculpt a concrete statue of Fr. Junipero Serra below the courthouse in 1937 as a project of the federal Works Project Administration (WPA). The statue remained for 50 years but was so badly deteriorated that, in 1990, it was replaced with the present-day bronze statue. A carved wooden statue, used as the mold, stands in the atrium of city hall.

Ventura pioneer Sol N. Sheridan is pictured standing by the Father Serra statue in the late 1930s. Visible in the background of the image is the Ewing House on the corner of Poli and Chestnut Streets. Homes built during the Victorian era were typically a reflection of the owner's wealth and social status. The wealthier one was, the larger the house.

The Bradley House, shown in the vintage image, was located on South Palm Street. John Hardin Bradley and Nellie Newby Bradley arrived in Ventura in 1871 and started the first newspaper in Ventura County, the *Ventura Signal*, from this house. The El Patio Hotel, built in the 1930s, is located on the site of the old Bradley House. Many Bradley family descendants still reside locally.

The Solari House was located at the corner of Figueroa and Meta Streets. The family emigrated from Italy and joined the Schiappapietra family as business associates. Both families were quite wealthy as demonstrated by the homes they built. Today a large commercial building is located on busy Thompson Boulevard (formerly Meta Street).

IN AND AROUND DOWNTOWN

This vintage 1890s view of the Peirano House shows that little has changed between then and now. The Queen Anne home was built in 1895 for Nick Peirano's new bride. In the 1970s, the house was abandoned but was purchased by a local attorney and restored. The small Australian tea tree shown in the vintage image is now very large.

Ventura had a true Italian mansion built by Federico and Antonio Schiappapietra in 1876. The towering mansion had 18 rooms, a white marble fireplace, and high ceilings decorated with plaster relief cherubs and angels. Located on Santa Clara Street between Figueroa and Palm Streets, the house was bulldozed in 1953 to put in a city parking lot.

The vintage image shows the westerly entrance into Ventura around 1928. There was no freeway, and old-timers remember traveling across the Ventura River Bridge to Garden Street, around Salad Bowl Curve, to the U.S. 101 Business District. Today this portion of the road is mainly used as a way to connect to Highway 101 North from downtown.

Ventura's "modern" fire station is featured in the vintage image from the 1940s. Located on the corner of Figueroa and Santa Clara Streets, it housed two pumper trucks, a hydraulic aerial ladder truck, spacious living quarters, and a five-story practice tower. Today an upscale lounge, Hush, shares space with the Clocktower Inn in the old fire station.

Ventura loves its parades, and this Fourth of July celebration confirms that. The building behind the vehicles is the Paul Hornung Harness and Saddles shop at the corner of Oak and Main Streets. Parked on the street to the left are buggies. The pennants announce "Celebrate July 4-5 at Ventura." The building today houses American Apparel.

This wide shot of Main Street, near Oak Street, has not changed much since the vintage image was taken in the 1930s or 1940s. The saddle shop was replaced with a Rexall Drug Store and in the now image houses American Apparel. Ventura's downtown is known for its nostalgic small-town feel.

4

MISCELLANEOUS
STREET SCENES

As depicted in this view from the 1880s, Ventura was very rural. The heart of town still remained close to the mission, with small farms and large agricultural operations farther east. With no landmarks clearly visible, the location of this photograph is difficult to determine. It is believed to be the intersection of Hemlock and Santa Clara Streets, because in the far right are headstones in Saint Mary's Cemetery. The cemetery (now a park) is located near Main and Hemlock Streets.

This is the John F. Binns House, which stood at 247 South California Street. The Binns family owned it from 1906 to 1956, when it was razed to make way for the freeway. Longtime residents remember when one could walk from downtown straight to the beach and the bluffs. The now location is air space over the northbound lanes of Highway 101.

North of the Binns house was the Hotel La Barr, which boasted "all outside rooms, all with baths, garages, and free parking" for the unheard of price of $2.00–$2.50. The hotel was torn down due to undermining caused by freeway grading. The building shown today housed a Carrows Restaurant for years, then a motorcycle shop, and now a clothing outlet.

HOTEL LA BARR — Dick Collins, Owner
Ventura, California
All outside rooms — All with bath — Double $2.00-$2.
Garages   Free Parking

The vintage 1950s shot of California Street shows the Taft Hotel and Astor Hotel on the left. The front facade of the Taft Hotel was designed by famed architect Albert C. Martin. Today the Taft is the Bella Maggiorre Inn, a popular bed and breakfast. Their resident ghost is named Sylvia, and she enjoys guests in her room (No. 17).

One of Ventura's original firehouses stood on California Street near the corner of Santa Clara Street. From its small beginnings as the Monumental Monitors in 1875, Ventura's fire department has evolved into a full-service department with six fire stations across town. The current location shows the California Street Mini Park.

This image from the April 1909 *Ventura Signal* shows the Union National Bank at Main and California Streets. The mule team is preparing Main Street for paving. The bank was torn down and replaced with the present building, originally another bank. That building is now known as the Erle Stanley Gardner Building; Gardner had an office on the third floor and penned the first Perry Mason novels there.

City hall was on the corner of California and Main Streets in this mission-style building with a library on the second floor. The Angel of Temperance (Ventura was a dry town) was actually a drinking fountain, and confiscated bootleg alcohol was dramatically poured down city drains. City hall was torn down and the Hotel Ventura built in 1926.

CITY HALL AND PUBLIC LIBRARY. VENTURA, CAL.

The Sheridan House was located near the top of California Street below Poli Street (on the left). It was torn down and a new building constructed to house the Pioneer Museum, which had been operating in the basement of the courthouse.

When the new museum opened on Main Street, the California Street building housed county offices, and it now houses City Corps, a youth volunteer organization.

Judge Ewing, one of Ventura County's earliest judges, built this home in 1894 on the corner of Poli and Chestnut Streets. Next to the Ewing house is the D. J. Reese House and the Bard Hospital. Today the Ewing house is a law office, and Poli Street no longer features the palm trees that once lined both sides. Poli Street is a scenic drive that turns into Foothill Road and makes for a pleasant jaunt.

Elizabeth Bard Memorial Hospital.
Ventura, Cal.

The Elizabeth Bard Memorial Hospital, built in 1901, is located above Poli Street at Fir Street. It was the town's first modern hospital. Dr. Cephas Little Bard became ill shortly after the hospital opened and died in his own hospital. Today the hospital is leased office space, and the good doctor's ghost frequently makes himself known.

The view down Fir Street has not changed much in the past 100 years. The roof peaks of Plaza School are visible in the vintage image. Homes in this area of downtown are desirable for the breathtaking ocean view they afford. Over the past decade, there has been a resurgence of restoring older homes instead of tearing them down.

oking South on First Street, Ventura, Cal.

The view up Fir Street, taken in the 1920s, shows the Jones House on the right sporting a large wraparound porch. This is a typical tree-lined street of its era. Today's image shows some change; most notably, the Jones House has undergone significant remodeling. Today a popular eatery named Bernadette's is located in the house.

Lovely old Victorian homes once graced Main Street, as shown in the vintage image taken from Fir Street looking east. The Jones House is on the corner, with the Capt. David Blackburn House next door. Captain Blackburn was a Civil War veteran and local businessman. Many houses are gone, but Main Street still retains its charm.

The two-and-a-half story Plaza School was built in 1888 on the corner of Fir and Santa Clara Streets. It housed a grammar school on the first floor and the high school on the second floor. It was torn down in 1932, when the present-day U.S. Post Office was built.

The vintage image shows the old Spanish cannon in its original location in Plaza Park. San Buenaventura is inscribed on the cannon, which dates to the late 1700s and came from the Philippines. It was found at the San Francisco Presidio and brought back to Ventura. In the current image, the large tree is a Moreton Bay fig planted in the 1870s.

An unidentified group of youngsters in costume celebrate the Fourth of July, possibly commemorating Adm. Robert Peary's expedition to the North Pole, since they look a bit snow-covered. Note the houses in the background along Chestnut Street. The Moreton Bay fig tree is in its infancy. Today there are no residential homes on the west side of Plaza Park.

The City of Ventura seemed to have quite a few city halls; this building is on Santa Clara Street near Chestnut Street. This image was taken in the 1960s, and about 10 years later in 1974, Ventura found its last city hall when the county courthouse was purchased from the County of Ventura. Today Affinity Bank is located in this building.

Plaza School, originally at this location on Santa Clara Street and Fir Street, was sold to the U.S. government for $41,900 and torn down to make way for a modern post office. This beautiful 1930s building was modernized around the 1950s. In the lobby of the post office are beautiful murals done as a WPA project that are well worth seeing.

The view up Chestnut Street from Santa Clara Street shows old Victorian and Craftsman homes. At the corner of Main and Chestnut Streets stands the Rose Hotel, and diagonally across from it is the back of Mercer's Garage. Chestnut Street is now commercial businesses on the left and, on the right, mid-block, is the Ventura Theater, built in 1928.

The large house on the corner of Kalorama and Santa Clara Streets is still there, it just can't be seen. It was moved to the back of the parcel when the Spanish-style Horizon Foursquare Church was constructed in the 1940s. The Victorian house was remodeled to make it fit with the Spanish architecture; the matching windows reveal the secret.

RESIDENCE VENTURA CAL

Main Street then was just as busy as Main Street now. In the right foreground of the vintage image are the grounds of the E. P. Foster Library. On the corner where present-day Dargan's is located, an old Union Oil Company building sits. The old cafés and small hotels are gone, replaced by retail shops.

A favorite pastime for locals and tourists is to travel up to Grant Park for breathtaking panoramic views of Ventura, both the coastline and up the Ventura Avenue area. The vintage shot from the 1940s shows the avenue (formerly called the Ventura River Valley) slowly becoming more residential with some remaining farmland.

This early 1960s view to the west shows a recently opened U.S. Highway 101. Completion of the highway was a double-edged sword: it provided easier travel, but it also passed through Ventura, cutting into the tourist trade. Getting the exact same angle was a little difficult due to vegetation growth.

The *c.* 1895 Chaffee House stood at the corner of Kalorama and Main Streets. Descendants fondly recall roller-skating in the round turret at the top of the house. The house was moved to the end of California Street and then torn down when the Holiday Inn (now Crowne Plaza Hotel) was built. Today the hillside is completely covered in homes.

The First Christian Church occupied the corner of Main and Laurel Streets and is a prime example of preservation through adaptive reuse. The Rubicon Theatre opened in the church in 1999 and presents acclaimed productions throughout the year.

The 1928 image shows the corner of Main and Ash Streets as all residential homes. The Ventura Elks Lodge was built during the same year and was purchased by the Becker Group several years ago. The building is in the midst of restoration and is available for public use.

MIDTOWN TO MONTALVO

Entering Ventura was like the caption of this vintage photograph postcard from around the 1920s. Main Street was still planted with palm trees and had not been widened yet. In the distance was the spire of the Rose Hotel. Now the palm trees are long gone and in the lot on the left, just past the parked vehicle, is an elementary school. Ventura was originally called the "Palm City" but is now officially the "Poinsettia City." The population was about 8,000.

The vintage image of St. Mary's Cemetery was taken in the 1960s for a high school photography project. The earliest portion, St. Mary's, dates to 1862. In 1889, a Protestant section was established, and in 1895, a Hebrew section was established. The cemetery was abandoned in the 1940s, and the headstones were removed in the 1960s. Today it is called Memorial Park, but the locals call it Cemetery Park.

The vintage photograph shows a 1903 St. Louis "horseless carriage" in front of the McCandliss house on the corner of Crimea and Poli Streets.

The large beautiful house still graces that corner and sits above Cemetery Park.

In recent years, a tremendous amount of controversy has arisen over what should be done with the cemetery/park. A design consultant drafted plans for a cemetery/park renovation, but due to the economy and public outcry, the plans have been shelved. This view is looking across the cemetery/park toward Main Street. The church is two blocks over on Santa Clara Street.

The inscription on the back of the vintage photograph says, "Paving Poli 1928." Even during the 1920s, mule teams were utilized for street projects in Ventura. This block of homes is on Poli Street between Pacific and Catalina Streets. The majority of the homes remain today, and many have been beautifully restored.

Merle's Drive-In, a blast from the 1950s, was situated at Five Points, where Main Street, Telegraph Road, Thompson Boulevard, and Loma Vista Road intersect. The popular drive-in featured carhop service and root beer floats. Today Muntz Stereo is at the location, still catering to cars.

Distinctive *Side Car* Restaurant

How many vintage 1938 Pullman Dining Cars does one see as a restaurant? The Side Car on Main Street has been a landmark since the 1940s. Merle Afferbaugh, owner of Merle's Drive-In, also owned the Side Car. Over the years, it has been a variety of things, including an antique store and now an upscale restaurant.

The Mission Bell Motel harkens back to the days of motor lodges. Situated on Main Street near Dunning Street, it is another piece of Ventura's nostalgic past. During its heyday, the motel was surrounded by lemon orchards. The Mission Bell Café, barely visible to the right, was a popular eatery and has recently been reopened as McConnell's Ice Cream Parlor.

The old Community Memorial Hospital, originally E. P. Foster Memorial Hospital, was built in 1930 and stood on Loma Vista Road at the intersection of Dalton Street. This early 1960s view shows the maternity pavilion to the left. In 1962, the hospital was renamed Community Memorial Hospital. Eventually a brand-new hospital was built and the old hospital torn down.

Montalvo School was built on Grand Avenue in 1889. Montalvo was a farming community. In 1911, the school burned down, and a new school was built in its place. All through the years until the late 1990s, the "Montalvo Mound," seen in the background, was undeveloped. Now the mound is covered in large homes, condominiums, and apartment buildings.

Another rural school was Mound School, built some time in the 1880s. In Dorothy Jue Lee's *A History of the San Buenaventura School District*, the school was located at the intersection of Telephone Road and Highway 101. Without a Sanborn Map to show the exact location, it is presumed to have been near the present-day Barnes and Noble bookstore on Telephone Road.

This image is one of the most exciting images of East Ventura. The boy, Charles Cole, stands in a field of huge calla lilies. The Cole family farmed vast areas of Ventura and owned Cole Canyon at the upper end of Aliso Street in downtown. The field of lilies is present-day Buena High School on Telegraph Road and Victoria Avenue. Sexton Road is to the right alongside the trees and is now Victoria Avenue.

CHAPTER 6

WHEN PRESERVATION WORKS

The Dudley House was built in 1892 on Telegraph Road and modern-day Ashwood Street. The family raised lima beans, walnuts, and lemons on 200 acres for decades. The house is a fine example of the simple farmhouses that dotted Ventura's landscape.

Until the Dudley House was moved in 1977, it stood on Telegraph Road and present-day Ashwood Street. After the house was moved, the site was home to Bob's Big Boy for decades but has since become Carrows Restaurant.

Owned by the City of Ventura since 1977, the Dudley House was moved to its present location at the corner of Loma Vista and Ashwood Streets. The vintage 1970s photograph shows the house being settled onto its basement foundation.

The nonprofit San Buenaventura Heritage Association has lovingly cared for and restored the Dudley House since 1978. It has taken thousands of volunteer hours and buckets of sweat to transform it into the treasure it is today. This is the view of the stairway coming in from the front door.

After the house was settled onto the basement foundation, the entire interior was stripped down to bare wood and restored. The Dudley House is one of the best examples of how a community can work together to preserve its heritage. The Dudley House docents offer home tours the first Sunday of each month and participate in numerous outreach events.

Looking from the parlor into the dining room, Miriam Dudley—portrayed by docent Modenia Kramer—sips a cup of tea as she welcomes guests into her dining room. Costumed docents lead visitors throughout the house and take them back to the days of lima beans and lemon groves.

Another historic home preserved for posterity is the Olivas Adobe on Olivas Park Drive. The Monterey-style adobe home was built by Don Raymundo Olivas in 1847. It was located on what was known as Rancho San Miguel, a rancho of nearly 5,000 acres. The house was sold in 1899 to the Alvords and in the 1920s to Max Fleischmann. After Fleischmann's death, the house was gifted to the City of Ventura.

This is a photograph of *la sala* (the living room). Originally the house was heated with a potbelly stove; the large fireplace was added after the Olivas family sold the house. The house is reportedly haunted by several ghosts and, in taking a few now photographs, an orb appeared on one image. Is it a ghost orb? The Olivas Adobe is popular during Halloween for ghost hunts.

WHEN PRESERVATION WORKS

In the corner of the courtyard is a small adobe. It is thought to have been used as sleeping quarters for the Olivas boys. Current restoration efforts call for this adobe to become an interactive display of life at the adobe from the 1860s through the 1950s.

www.arcadiapublishing.com

Discover books about the town where you grew up, the cities where your friends and families live, the town where your parents met, or even that retirement spot you've been dreaming about. Our Web site provides history lovers with exclusive deals, advanced notification about new titles, e-mail alerts of author events, and much more.

Find Your Place in History.